NOBODY

Faith Lavon

Nobody Knows But God

Series One Vol 1

Faith Lavon

Published by Actor's Ground, 2019.

NOBODY KNOWS BUT GOD

First edition. December 16, 2019.

ISBN: 978-1393644620

Written by Faith Lavon.

Table of Contents

NOBODY KNOWS BUT GOD ....

VOID ....

FIRST FELT HURT...

INAPPROPRIATE ....

PAPA .... 1(

INNER GIRL 1

CRY 1

RUN RUN RUNNING .... 1(

SWEET ROXANN.. 1

SHE'S UNFORGIVEN.. 18

HYPOCRITE .... 1!

ISN'T THAT WHAT THEY SAY.. 2

UNSHED TEARS .... 2.

POTION 2

SEARCHING FOR MAMA .... 2(

HE AND SHE... 28

REMEMBER ME 29

CLEARLY LOVE... 31

MY MAN.. 33

SHE AND HE 36

CREEPY LOVE 37

BITCH 38

LONELY PEOPLE 40

BEGINNING 42

SUNSET 43

LOVE CONDITIONAL 45

MOON MOTHER 46

DEAREST 48

IT'S NOT ME 50

NOTHING BUT LIGHT 51

I AM 52

IT'S JUST 53

SHE WONDERED 55

HIM 57

THE MOMENT I KNEW 58

DONE 60

PRECIOUS ROAD 61

I ALMOST DROWNED 62

INSIDIOUS ANGER 64

IN PLACE 66

FAMILIAR..68

BEAUTIFUL DISTRACTIONS..70

EMERGE..72

WAITING...73

BOTTOMLESS..75

HOLD STEADY..77

I AM STRENGTH AGAIN..79

TOP OF THE BOTTOM...81

LESSON LEARNED...83

MY HEARTS...84

I want to dedicate this book to Ashley and Asia Collins. You girls are a continuous inspiration to me.

NOBODY KNOWS BUT GOD

Nobody knows but God

where I awoke this morning;

I awoke to disbelief.

Our home wasn't home,

but a cave of lonely diseases.

Was not home because we didn't make it one.

Nobody knows but God

that I lay looking above,

watching strangled flies in cobwebs.

My face strangled by poverty,

My structure distorted,

My strength weaves.

Hold on to disbelief

Only way to survive

Nobody knows but God

that roaches crawl across my face as I sleep

Or that the fleas feed on my sweet blood.

No water

No food;

Moldy dishes from both.

Nobody knows but God

that every morning he empties

a bucket of piss in the backyard,

Refills with fresh water from the hose next door

To relieve in

To bathe in

To drink from

Nobody knows but God

that candles light our darkness.

My shadows are drained

My soul lags, but my faith survives

the tortures of reality;

The faces of disbelief grin and wave

Nobody knows but God

That a strained smile often fails.

A glimmer of hope smothered,

Withstanding this affliction,

Pacifying this ailment

I can't seem to grasp my way out.

Nobody knows but God

why I'm here.

VOID

Am I crazy?

No

I can see perfectly clear

I

Sometimes my visions explode

Each piece is a new story

The daylight isn't daylight

It's just night masked by the rotting elements we know nothing about

Am I crazy?

No

I can see perfectly clear

I

I'm in a place called Void

Emotions that surge but held prisoner

Where do you put them?

Bury them or do you lay them in the daylight to rot?

Am I crazy?

No

I can see perfectly clear

I

You tricked me

I believed

Void

Creatures invade my spirit

Fighting hard

Bars of the prison will not release me

Always fighting

Am I crazy?

No

I can see perfectly clear

I

God help me

I am crazy

Void

FIRST FELT HURT

As I walked behind them

the glare of the morning sun shines

It bounces off my face

As I walked behind them

I glared at the back of their heads

He gives her one more bolster up

to secure her in his arms

As I walked behind them

they moved to the left revealing the surprise

The brown metallic of the semi truck sparkles

She squeals in delight

as she sees her name on the front

I looked down at the sidewalk

Wondering why am I here?

It feels like I'm intruding on a special moment

meant just for them

I'm the first grandbaby

But she's the baby

I feel a pain in my heart

It aches and pounds in my ears

Why am I here?

I'm invisible to them

Why am I here?

INAPPROPRIATE

they touched me inappropriately

then he touched me inappropriately

then he touched her inappropriately

it hurt her I could tell

he tried to make me touch him inappropriately

but I escaped

but he made my sister touch him inappropriately

it hurt her I could tell

he kissed me inappropriately

his gritty tongue in my mouth

then he touched me inappropriately

I can't

then I told

he is gone

then he made me feel like I was his

but I wasn't

then he said I was pretty made up

but not so much without

then he hollered at me

I ignored him

he berated me

you not that cute bitch

then I loved him

then I sent my baby back

I was hurt

I could tell

then he said nice things

so I chased him

yearned for them, him

then I Am made Himself known

He knew me

He knows me

I Am loves me purely

am I pure again?

I want to be pure again

purely pure this time

PAPA

papa

pops

father

not much

my hand in the jelly jar

caught behind the couch

booming voice

my little body trembles with fear

mama hit

grandmas broomstick

mama hit again and again

mama hit

mama pushes daddy over the porch banister

I squeal in delight at mama's bravery

I am brave now

no more bully her

no more bully me

I am brave now too

babysitter, his wife

babysitter's son, my brother

he says, don't let that truck scare you

I am brave now so brave

I drift towards the truck

he grabs the wheel

I squeal with delight inside

I scared him

I am brave now

he doesn't scare me now

went to soon

gone before he went

daddy

father

not much

pops

oh papa

INNER GIRL

My inner girl sings

pleading for God to hear my voice

Sunflower breeze

Kansas wheat

Crawdaddy creek wraps the field

The well water runs deep

Mud pies made with love

The gravel road beats under my bare feet

Blackberries stain my fingers

Angels dance around the tree

watching me sleep

The snake swims on top of the pitts

The wasp stings

It's my turn to stomp the greens

and hang the clothes dry

Wild rabbit and gravy with beer biscuit aromas

Buttons our dog stands ten feet tall

Coffee with Fannie my favorite thing

Roasted tomatoes on top of the stove

Cucumbers in jars turns into pickles

Back outside looking up at the sky

My inner girl sings once again

praying for God to hear my song

CRY

I don't cry

Surging plunging

I go beyond the realms of my dreams

to see the wall of my Leo moon

I drown

Dry

I don't cry

There's something missing

My heart beats, it drips

Indulging in fantasy is not an option

My will cracks it, it tears, shatters it

No tears

Dark is the reflection you can't see in the mirror

I don't cry

Warped visions heal

Tormented souls dance to classical music

A rigid heart and mind

Makes a spirit lag in logic

Weep

Just washing my eyes

Really I don't cry

Not knowing is a rough surface

Knowing is knowledge wrapped in a bun tightly

Pain pain go away

and agonize my soul another day

I don't cry

RUN RUN RUNNING

I sent him on a wild run after me

Through mazes

Through trees

Through bushes

To the cage

He sent his friend running ahead of me

He started to slow his pace

I almost ran into myself

I looked back to see him stopping

I knew what he had planned

But I stopped anyway

Concerned

He grabbed me

We fell to the ground

His front to my back

Underneath the light

Whispering securities, and I melted

Just melted

As his friend stood watching

SWEET ROXANN

Sweet Roxann

My Scorpion Queen

I miss your Halston smell

and your eyes of hollow brown

Your sting of guarded love

is my power to strive for excellence

Dear ma mère

My sugar rose

You're wilting as I grow

Your lovely pedals

They were sold

You disappeared through the fogginess

of my realities

Yet you remain in my stilted dreams

In the lake of my agonies, you lay afloat

as I wait and wait for your

shiftless return

SHE'S UNFORGIVEN

She's unforgiven

Because she left me

But did I not do the same?

Secrets untold

Secrets telling

Emotions seem to be numb

How is it that she's unforgiven?

Because she left me

But did I not do the same?

Once in a while

I feel like cussing

When things are spinning too fast

Running is a gift I have

that was given to me by she

How is it that she's unforgiven?

Because she escaped

But did I not do the same?

HYPOCRITE

Hypocrite I

I the hypocrite

I said this

But I did that

I speak before I think

I think before I speak

Contradiction

I don't even practice

what I teach

I rule and dictate

then do as I please

My brain is laughing

because my heart is lapping

in the exposure of truth

Hypocrite I

I the hypocrite

I say surrender

Then I board my insides

with a hard shell of fears

With no escape except

a smile through

well deserved tears

Fighting for substance

I plunge into delirium

Because my soul is gone

Gone for a time

into another fairytale

ISN'T THAT WHAT THEY SAY

Don't run away from your fears

Let go of yesterday

Is what they say

My father said he'd never get old

Now he's turning old in his grave

Is what they say

The blind man can see

The seeing man is blind

The round world is flat

What comes around goes around,

Isn't that what they say?

Grit your teeth when you get mad

Count to ten when you get mad

Is what they say

The peace sign means war

Yellow light means go

Is what they say

The rich man is poor

The poor man still poor

Someone said be all that you can be

But I'm struggling hard to just be me,

Isn't that what they say?

Trust and honesty

Is the key

Is what they say

Values and morals

Diamonds and pearls

Iss what they say

Man and wife

Wife and wife

Man and man

Monkey see, monkey do

Isn't that what they say?

UNSHED TEARS

When I see them in the morning time

I can hear their anguish in my ears

My sister asking for some change

for her evening meal

Unshed tears lay where they lay

Brother man no place to stay

Can you feel passion race my heart?

Soul to soul emotions ripe

All so clear my mind surges

As your soul tears mine apart

Unshed tears roll away

Getting old everyday

Our dignities lay stain

Our lonely hearts just creep away

So ashamed of what we see

Where did the love go?

Show up

Oh my God

POTION

Washing her naked form

she floats in a superb plain of pleasure

The potion distracts her memories

Intriguing them to come alive

Looking and flickering

Lathering she tries to forget them

They wag their tails

Greedy for more wood on the fire

She rests her head against the tub

She closes her eyes and images leap to

the sound of the dripping potion

Mesmerized by the dancing blackness

of white light she withdrawals

She then stares into open air reflecting her

pale patterns of unnourished love

Her teardrops fall to mix with the silky potion

that has created a new world

However familiar

Dreary thoughts lead her to believe

that the bath is over

SEARCHING FOR MAMA

Always searching for Mama

Looking for her, through her

Tugging at dresses and having tea

Perhaps the church lady will be

Step right up mother potential

I'll meet you at Macy's at three

Maybe she's sitting at the beach next to my being

I can call her mama possibly

Teacher teacher pick she

Granny is a great substitute

Auntie the next best thing

I'm not sure where to go next

I've looked at the highest peak

I've looked through the underbelly

Then a thought rises gently

Maybe mother is inside of me

Borrowing time until I have my own

There she is

I can see her finally,

In the mirror, she is me

HE AND SHE

He smiled at her

Just a simple smile

Her eyes told him

that's all she needed

He touched her

Just simply touched her

Her body told him

that's what she wanted

He made love to her

like dancing flames

She steadily fed the fire

with her lips against his chest

The fire spoke loudly and vigorously

The fire spoke softly and viciously

The fire reached its climax

Then died down

but left a spark

to be rekindled for the next time

REMEMBER ME

Silence drips from the wall

in a horrible elegance of silk

that blows uncontrollably through the

blackness of my mind

Remember me.

To smell the blueness of the sky

you must taste the earth

To feel the cloud

you must rip the lining

To bathe in the light

you must sacrifice the sun

The blackness from the cup

can see my staggered appearance

Remember me.

No answer

Caress the shoulder of the bare form

Feel the silk, but be cautious of the web

Baby don't cry

Daddy will hum you a lullaby

Remember me.

Can't see

Blackness sees you in the true form

of your selfishness

Guide me to the boat that will set sail

for the sky, the clouds, and the sun

Silence drips

Remember me.

CLEARLY LOVE

Love

Love

A dreamy state

Love

Hanging on edge

Love so unfocused, but strong

Love

Love

Waves of sparkling crystals

Love

A white puffy cloud

Love

Simply complexed

Love

Love

A magic carpet

Love

Plain pain sometimes

Love

Pleasures of all kinds

Love

Love

Fear, feared, fearing

Love

Whirl of worlds

Love

My soul, the soul

Love

Love

Sounds of the echo

Love

Pleading for an entrance

Love

Crawling towards an exist

Love see

Clearly

See love

Love

Love

MY MAN

my man

my love man

chocolate man

lover man

he soothes

he sweats

earth man

cool man

he's vain

sometimes

sexy man

my beautiful man

touch me man

want you man

real bad man

come man

to me

he's cool

always cool

body man

man body

that tongue man

does a lot man

need I say more man

tough man

my rough man

rigid man

in my dreams man

in my heart

man what you do to me

man oh boy

my man

he smiles

my heart stops

breathe breathe

my confident man

sweet man

strong man

your mouth

your eyes

your face

your skin

so smooth

so nice

lovely to feel man

he looks in the mirror

always

go ahead smile man

all this true

all this mine

so proud

so very proud

that you are my man

SHE AND HE

She said kiss me quick

He did

She said love me

He did

He said kiss me slowly

She did

He said love me

She did

Communication and honesty is survival

It's the sole key to all openings

CREEPY LOVE

You know creepy love

Open, all open

Women you know that creepy love

Seesaw

Up and down

Rollerblade ride down the hill

Zig zagging reacting

Reaching to share

One way only

Your doing of course

Control sounds familiar

Not your doing of course

Creepy love

Strange love to have

Games a plenty

Just plain creepy love

You know

BITCH

Bitch

He called me

Bitch

My mother called me

Bitch

He says things to hurt me

To upset me

She says things to confuse me

To stop me from

Bitch

My mother called me

Bitch

He called me

Bitch

Sweet rose

That hurts

I love him

I love her

They love me

Yes you do

I hate you

I love you

Bitch

He called me

Bitch

My mother called me

Bitch

LONELY PEOPLE

The two lonely people ride in silence

He, grim and hard

She, nonchalantly looks at the newspaper

No words

So very close, so very far

Is it love or hate or both?

The two lonely people create tension

The friction is overwhelming

We love her for being so strong

We dislike him for being so strong

Her strength is radiant and glossed over

His strength, a weakness he doesn't understand

I'm bias towards her

I see what I see

The two lonely people

Have no communication

The passion has vanished

The eyes say no more

There is a rancid growth rendering

their relationship useless

The growth has a mind of its own

Controlling all thoughts

and bleeding the heart and soul dry

The two lonely people

Have nothing in common

Except the hollow emptiness

that forms a circle around them

Separate lives

Separate shadows

Separate

Just separate

BEGINNING

He is

He was

He showed me from the beginning

I saw

I've seen

I've known from the beginning

Red flags like ladybugs in a garden

White flags like droplets of dew

Waving slow

Waving faster

Waving vigorously

Come get me

Scoop me up

Take me to a new beginning

SUNSET

The sunrise lies

The sunset sees truth beginning

When it's dark, you can't see the filth of light

dawning on a city of facades

How cruel the light can be

So focused on teaching good

There is no hallucination about darkness

Our friend evil and bad rule that dominion

with a tricky solitude of unspoken grace

Such faith in their empire

Frightening it is

The light tells horrible tales

Hello

Hello

How are you

Fine

How are you

Fine

Doesn't that sound heavenly

Evil loves to capture a contorted soul

His brother darkness

feeds on the mystery of a hideous frown

Smile smile smile so vile

Interesting isn't it

Shadows exist in the light

These lovely creatures are only foreplay

to the devious creation of our sister wicked

Which would you prefer?

The hidden agendas of the sunrise

or the divine pleasures of the sunset

LOVE CONDITIONAL

Conditional love

Conditions of my love

Conditions with my love

Conditions in spite of my love

Conditions to my love

to receive my love

to hold my love

to respect my love

Conditions of love based on behavior

on merit

on words

on memories

on last week

Reckless conditions of love

Cruel conditions of love

Unfair conditions of love

Conditions may be the hand that's dealt

Condition yourself to deal with the hand

MOON MOTHER

Align me Moon Mother with your mystery

Glide over my heart with your hair of herbs

to blind the broken beat of my skipping machine

My self esteem slipping

I thought I had a grip so unyielding

But like sand held too tightly

it escaped my hand,

to blend in with

to search for the others like me

Oh lovely Moon Mother,

save me

Lend me your spirit of truth so that I may

grow stronger in your absence

Oh Moon Mother

My generous Queen

Hear and see the tears flowing to gather at my feet

drowning in helplessness and pity

Please I'm speaking

My echo swarming and ready to take me

inside hysteria if I go

Moon Mother

They won't let me return to you

Listen,

hear me calling

DEAREST

Dearest darling

I gave you the benefit of the doubt

Even as you sought answers to use against

Beloved man

I gave you the secret part of me

Even though you fed me to the wolves

Warmest heart

I gave you the remedy to uphold love

Even when you dug in with all fours

Sweet fellow

I gave you your fondest moments

Even when I saw you running in your stance

Tender soul

I gave you a sublime platter of choices

Even though you flipped the tray in judgments

Charming boy

I gave you clear alternatives

Even though it was never enough

Lovely angel

I gave you the ingredients to soar

Even as you took for granted I'd always be there

Sugar honey

I'm not so strong anymore

The knew has turned into knowing

IT'S NOT ME

Is it me?

Maybe it's me

Could be me

Uh um no

It's you

It's definitely you

NOTHING BUT LIGHT

The light is staring

Staring right at me

Right through me

Nothing to offer but a sad face

A lonely frustrated heart

Full of life ready to share

To give up hope

for you to show up

The bright light warms my face

The light could make me see

the tunnel of my inner misery

I can see you peeking behind the light

You, the force which penetrates me,

looks to see if the bait is in my mouth

It is

The mirror was right this morning

I'm a fool

I AM

I am

I am

I am

I am

I am

I am

Am I doubting

I am

IT'S JUST

It's the micro things that you say

It's the passive aggressive maneuvering that you do

It's the loss of hearing when I speak

It's the credit that you take

It's the credit that you don't give

It's the credit that you seek

It's the love that you hold hostage

It's the arm that you use as a shield

It's the downward arrow of your brow

It's the blame that you spew

It's the blame that you refuse to take

It's the blame that you cover over me

It's the judgement that you voice

It's the judgement of silence that I hear

It's the judgement like your stuff don't stink

It's the way that you think

It's the way that you speak to me

It's the way that you laugh at me

It's the way that you disrespect me

It's the how that you ignore

It's the how that you continuously dismiss

It's the how that you have issues with

It's your arrogance that astounds me

It's your insecurities that's staggering

It's too late to fix

It's too late to save

It's just not worth it anymore babe

SHE WONDERED

As she looked across the tip of the mountain

she wondered what pleases him

As she looked down the crooked path

she wondered what pleases him

As the sun set and the moon took its place

she wondered what pleases him

As she danced in the moonlight beams

she wondered what pleases him

As she slept and bathed in her fantasies

she wondered what pleases him

As she birthed her babies into being

she wondered what pleases him

As she planned events of birthdays and dreams

she wondered what pleases him

As she gave thanks on Thanksgiving and

decorated the tree she wondered what pleases him

As she made a home from nothing and

cooked his favorite things she wondered what pleases him

As she pretended his touch was still good and wanted

she wondered if it would soon be over

She delayed and delayed, waited and postponed

Then gave up and gave in to her new adventures alone

HIM

When I met Him who gave life

I was a weakened tormented soul

When I met Him who was love

I was so deeply moved that I transformed

When I met Him who talked and walked with me

I felt so pure, so empowered

When I met Him who whispered encouragement

I felt like a Queen, a pillar of strength

When I met Him who looked straight through me

I felt free and peacefully complete by Him

When I met Him he had always

been there cascading around me

I just needed to invite Him in

THE MOMENT I KNEW

I stood in the living room

looking through you

The light breeze of truth floods my senses,

the moment I knew

But I insisted and pushed

I presented the case that we were meant for us

I stood in the living room

looking through you

The light of truth permeated through the winter window,

the moment I knew

But I persisted and pleaded

I decorated the tray for you to see what our lives could be

I stood in the living room

looking through you

The thunder of truth rumbled through me,

the moment I knew

But I screamed and gleaned

I gathered the memories in a photo album, a song, a poem

I stood in the living room

looking through you

The reign of truth raining between us,

the moment I knew

But I danced and I cried

I filled the glass half full until it overflowed with emptiness

I stood in the living room

looking right through you

A sigh, a closing of the eyes, a breath

The truth on the other side

the moment I knew

the moments I knew

that moment I knew

That moment I saw through you

DONE

Over your head

Wow

You are actually

Damn

I'm done

PRECIOUS ROAD

Seeking

Seeking

Seeking my fortune

Searching for my precious road

No one knows until the end

Uncertainty and paranoia are my evil twins

Honesty and trust are my secret enemies

And you

But you

Confront your shadows

Enrapture your dreams

and find your precious road

I ALMOST DROWNED

I almost drowned waiting on you to catch up

At first treading lightly

Then treading a little faster

In hopes to encourage you to venture

I almost drowned constantly turning back to see

At first just a peek

Then peeking excessively

In hopes to encourage you to plunge

I almost drowned persistently giving with no return

At first plenty

Then with fervor

In hopes to encourage you to give back to me

I almost drowned relentlessly ignoring my exhaustion

At first sometimes

Then all the time

In hopes to encourage you to display your optimum

I almost drowned continuously propelling your ego

At first slowly

Then out of obligation

In hopes to encourage you to embody your dreams

I almost drowned perpetually disregarding my own wellbeing

At first it was fine

Then it wasn't

In hopes to encourage you to look beyond your own desires

I almost drowned hoping you would join our journey

At first with anticipation

Then with mundane sorrow

In hopes to encourage you to reject your fears

I almost drowned in your trepidations

I almost drowned in your anxieties

I almost drowned in the waiting

I almost drowned.

INSIDIOUS ANGER

Anger insidious

It festers inside of me

Not sure what to do

Run

Stop about face

Stay looking through to the other side

Not greener

Stop about face

Hello anger

Who keeps me captured

I try and I try and I try and I try

Release me

Trying to stand tall, upright

Look through, forward step

Breathe

Creating room for peace

Peace creating room for love

Love creating room for me

Me creating room to be

There She is

Here She is

She is here

IN PLACE

I was running to this time

In place

Not getting anywhere

The sweat on my brow is deceiving

My muscles ache from being used

In place

I'm headed out towards the next

Gearing up to begin

In place

Squinted eyes of determination

Flexing and stretching my mind to proceed

In place

Trying to break the barriers of lies

Catching my breath before I quit

In place

Just one step outside the circle

Just one step to the left

In place

Invisible shackles on my ankles

I pull ahead to be pulled back

In place

With fire in my lungs

I breathe in water from the air

It quenches me

I'm getting there

I'm almost there

In place

FAMILIAR

Familiar looks you in the eye

It holds your attention

Familiar convinces you to stay

It holds you captive

Familiar wants you to choose it

It holds you near

Familiar soothes you in the corner

It makes you look at the potential from afar

Familiar bribes you to keep quiet

It holds your mouth hostage

Familiar knows your darkness

It holds you as the thief

Familiar keeps you angry

It holds you as it's mark

Familiar doesn't tell you when it lies

It doesn't tell you when you need to let go

It doesn't tell you your core is enough

It doesn't tell you being in the light is good

It doesn't tell you being clamorous is a gift

It doesn't hearten your plight

It doesn't assist your aspirations

It keeps you in a trance

It keeps you motionless in your options

Familiar is not your friend

BEAUTIFUL DISTRACTIONS

Beautiful distractions are the meaningful moments

They are always welcomed with fondness

Beautiful distractions are the threads that unravel us

They are our lovers

They are our partners

They are our children

They are our projects

They are our "plan B through Z"

They are our doubts

They are our intentions

They are our beloved friends

They are our escape

They are our habits

They make us contrite

They make us weep

They make us beam

They make us forget who we are at the center

Beautiful distractions are the outer realm of us

As beautiful as they are

As tempting as they can be

They are not who we are

They are not our pursuits

They are just little kisses of gratitude

To help us to our journey's end

EMERGE

My heart sank to the depths of the dark ocean floor

My eyes swollen from the night before

I'm speechless

I'm almost to the mouth of the cave

I can see the light dart through the forest trees

I can see the greenery at the base

I can smell the breeze of sweetness

Yet I'm reaching and can't feel

I'm restrained by my own essence

My own strength is my struggle

Crossing the threshold I'm worn

Dragging my body towards defeat

Willing my will to refresh itself

I come to tainted terms

My heart re-emerges gasping for air

Only to question my presence there

WAITING

Waiting for an answer

I blink twice waiting

Waiting for a response

I shift from side to side

Waiting for you to engage

I turn my head to hear better

Waiting for you to commune

I am silent to hear your voice

Waiting for you to attempt kindness

I am ready to receive it

Waiting for you to press forward

I will my heart to stay open

Waiting for you to lean in

I lean past my limits

Waiting for you to catch me

I unshackle my tether

Waiting for you to aid our union

I prepare the landing

Waiting for you to be

I changed me

BOTTOMLESS

Paralyzed in movement

Resting in motion

Standing in forward movement

I'm familiar with this space

It's harming me

Unhinged I am

Hemorrhaging from the inside out

Slowly releasing my toxic notions

Looking in the mirror I see tattered edges folded back

Flapping easily in the wind

Being content in my quest for wisdom

I must increase my strength

I must allow my vulnerability to humble me

The familiar will choke out life

It has a way of keeping you in survival

Never landing thoughts that strangle

The unexplored me

The desires of me

The purpose of me

The core of me

The soul of me

The spirit of me

The heart of me must break free

so that I can understand the bottomless pit of me

HOLD STEADY

Broken mosaic of utter confusion

Shattered beyond recognition

Until it makes a new piece of duplicity

Mayhem of lies inside the frame

Wandering inside I see me screaming

So many colors trying to tell a story

Feeling lost in the beat of the chaos

Unhinging and teetering at an angle

Looking over the cliff to see how far

A gust of fresh air floods my senses

Reminding me of my purpose forward

The overflow of sadness trail down my cheeks

It pools at my collarbone center

Walking into my resolutions dedicated

Unwavering in my vulnerability

It gives me strength

I stand upright

I face the next turn in the road

I hear my own voice bellow my name

Holding steady I take the next step

I AM STRENGTH AGAIN

The morning dew smiles back at me

The bluest sky gives me a wink

The sunshine hugs me tightly

The top of the mountain ridge breathes life in

The trees gather secrets and decides which to whisper

The rhythm of the wind makes itself known

The booming sound between my ears reminds me it's hard to hear

My voice wary of the recall

Nevertheless shouting out to be heard

Straining to be believed in

Standing up to the indivisible pressure

It threatens to turn me into worthiness

My mind shifts to the open field of possibles

Seeing the beauty on top

Wondering what's underneath at the root that grounds me

I crave solitude within

I yearn for the quietness that supersedes understanding

The light then tickles my toes

It veers up through me

I am strength again

TOP OF THE BOTTOM

I'm almost to the top of the bottom

I've been suffocating right below it

I'm sure to be murky and unclean

I must regain my stamina to pull up through

For reaching level is a feat in itself

I must catch my breath to take in new

I'm ready to be in the space of nothing for as long as I can

Figuring out whether to go left or right or straight ahead

I'm so grateful to leave the tedious circle of repeated mistakes

Equipped with the word of He who whispers my name

I'm ready to bust the shaded corners

I'm ready to push the mourning off my back

I'm ready to choose each of my assured steps

Each minute, each hour, each day dedicated to life in full

Knowing that nothing is infallible

Trusting in my leeway of inclinations

The top of the bottom enlivens my whole

The top of the bottom invigorates my entirety

The top of the bottom is where I arise

Going after who I exact am

Undoubtedly, undeniably, and unquestionably anew

LESSON LEARNED

I pity me no more

My choices chose my path

Declining your instincts will do that

Ignoring the rights

Compromising the wrongs

Giving into false pride is daft at best

I listened to folks who didn't make time

Who accused me of self seeking conceit

I believed them subconsciously

So I stuffed me in a square

So many hoops dangling from me

I got tangled up in others illogic

Tripped up in their sadness, I buried my own

It made no sense to breach my silver lining

But there I was participating in my demise

Enough no more

Where I am letting go

Hard earned lesson embraced and learned

MY HEARTS

My first heart the beginning piece

My next heart the filling piece

My broken heart the ending piece

My baby turns her head to me

My baby baby rides with me

My babe doesn't trust me

She fights for her voice

She embraces her mind

He retreats

Baby she wants to take care of me

Baby baby she wants to protect me

Babe is silent

Her choice to be joyful is pleasing to see

Her aim to be free is so refreshing

He is difficult

I see baby accepting her power

I see baby baby tackling the box

I see him deflecting

You baby are the essence of the earth

You baby baby are light beams in the flesh

You babe are fading

My first heart be audacious in your discoveries

My next heart be gallant in pioneering

My broken heart reclaim your place

Let the end be the start

Don't miss out!

Visit the website below and you can sign up to receive emails whenever Faith Lavon publishes a new book. There's no charge and no obligation.

https://books2read.com/r/B-A-OVPK-TGVBB

BOOKS 2 READ

Connecting independent readers to independent writers.